Uncomplicating DEATH

GUIDANCE FOR LIFE'S GREATEST AND FINAL TEST

Chaplain Garry Hodges

Top Reads Publishing, Inc
Vista, California

Copyright © 2018 by Garry Hodges

All Rights Reserved. No part of this publication may be reproduced, stored in or introduced into a retrieval system, or transmitted in any form or by any means (electronic, mechanical, photocopied, recorded of otherwise), without the prior written permission of both the copyright owner and the publisher of this book, except by a reviewer who wishes to quote brief passages in connection with a review written for insertion in a magazine, newspaper, broadcast, website, blog or other outlet.

First Edition

ISBN: 978-0-9986838-5-0

Uncomplicating Death: Guidance for Life's Greatest and Final Test is published by: Top Reads Publishing, Inc., 1035 E. Vista Way, Suite 205, Vista, CA, 92084-4213 USA

For information please direct emails to: topreadspublishing@gmail.com or visit the website: www.TopReadsPublishing.com

Cover design, book layout and typography: Teri Rider & Associates

Printed in the United States of America

25 24 23 22 21 20 19 18   1 2 3 4 5 6 7 8 9

Please Note:
Stories in *Uncomplicating Death* are true. Names and other identifying details of patients and their families have been changed to protect the privacy of those involved.

Table of Contents

Introduction...1
How Our Life Experiences Inform Our
Views of Death..5
    Important Conversations............................6
    Getting Current...................................6

Needs of the Dying Person............................10
    Physical Needs: Providing Care and
    Managing Pain....................................11
    Severe Pain Management...........................13
    Emotional and Spiritual Needs....................13
    Maintaining Autonomy.............................14
    What to Expect...................................17
    Patient Needs: A Quick Reference..............18

Needs of the Caregivers..............................20
    Caregiving Together..............................20
    Telling Your Story...............................21
    Caregiver Needs: A Quick Reference............23

Lessons from a Hospice Chaplain......................26
    Comfort..27
    Finding Peace....................................29
    Timelines..30
    Seeing as Believing..............................32
    What Makes End-of-Life So Difficult?.............35

Life, Love, and Tomorrow.............................37
A Note From the Author...............................41
Acknowledgements.....................................43

Introduction

Life has given us a very clear understanding of death. It comes at the wrong time; it threatens who we are, our future, and our identity. It is a burden like no other, loaded with many demanding responsibilities and decisions. It takes us out of our comfort zone and we may feel a loss of control while trying to face the demands of such difficult circumstances. To help make sense of it all, people may decide to call on the assistance of a chaplain, someone who is trained to offer guidance, comfort, and support in the face of death and bereavement.

My journey of becoming a chaplain started in 1990 when my ten-year-old daughter was in an accident. I was working in construction as an asphalt paving contractor, and I rushed from work to be with my daughter in the Emergency Room. As I waited for my daughter's minor injuries to be attended to, I struck up a conversation with a young man who was also waiting outside the ER. Unfortunately, his situation was much more severe than mine; his loved one was in critical condition and he was scared. I did my best to offer him comfort and reassurance. It was a simple thing, really. I was a listening ear and a shoulder to cry on, but that conversation changed my life forever.

After I left the hospital that day, I couldn't stop thinking about that young man. I was grateful that I was there to comfort him and it made me realize that I had a real desire to offer that service to others. A week after my daughter's accident I walked into the Chaplain's office within the hospital and introduced myself to the Senior Chaplain. We talked at length about the responsibilities and functions of the position, and I knew I wanted to follow the path to becoming a chaplain. After completing the required clinical training over the next two years, I became a chaplain in May of 1992. I started out as a part-time chaplain at Tri-City Medical Center until, in 2008, I was offered a position as Hospice Chaplain and Bereavement Coordinator for Tri-City Hospice.

I have met so many incredible people along the way; encounters and conversations that will stay with me forever. While working closely with people struggling with grief, pain, and sorrow during end-of-life, I've come to see just how valuable life truly is. My first experience as the chaplain on duty is one I will never forget.

I was called into the ER before the deceased arrived to receive information from the medical staff. The man had suffered a heart attack at home while having an argument with his neighbor and had died on the way to the hospital. I was asked to be present when his body arrived and offer comfort to the spouse and the rest of the family once they reached the hospital. The paramedics placed the deceased in an empty ER room. I was informed that the spouse had been contacted and was waiting for her family to bring her to the hospital. It would be an hour before they arrived to say their goodbyes. In the meantime, I was left alone with the deceased.

Twenty-four years later, the hour I spent alone with that decedent is still fresh in my memory. The experience was introspective in many ways. I wondered to myself why he still had his slippers on his feet. It quickly occurred to me that when he put his slippers on that morning, he had no idea he would not be the one removing them. To this day, I often think about that man when I put on my shoes. When I do, it is a gentle reminder to live in the light, and to live graciously, knowing this day could be my last. When I start the day with this in mind, I am more present, grateful, and open to life's possibilities.

Dying, death, and bereavement are all difficult experiences we will face in life. May your grief, pain, and sorrow not rob you of this day or tomorrow. Instead, I hope you will see that death can be as precious as it is painful. Each person's experience with death will be unique and complex. A Hospice Chaplain can be helpful to people in bereavement as they try to navigate the difficult trials initiated by transitions from life to death. This booklet contains insights and tools that can be applied before, during, and in the wake of death. I hope it will help guide you, comfort you, and encourage you on your own unique journey.

Uncomplicating Death

May you be guided through the storm;

Tossed about the sea with its deep unknown.

May you be guided to the harbor, calm and norm.

May you find rest with those you've known;

May you, together, be home-sick in;

Your journey to that place you've never been.

~ Chaplain Garry Hodges

How Our Life Experiences Inform Our Views of Death

At some point in our lives, we all eventually have an encounter with death. No matter what age we are when that first encounter occurs, there begins a real, deep, and lasting impression of death.

There are many factors we encounter almost daily that tend to inform our views on this subject: the news, movies and television, someone sharing the death of their loved one, witnessing a tragedy or an accident, the illness of a loved one, and even a life-threatening situation of our own.

During our lifetime, we develop scenarios for our own end-of-life and death scene which are influenced by our experiences with death. Over the years, our hopes and fears about death may change based on the experiences we have along the way. It is completely normal to imagine these things and it can be very powerful to talk about these ideas with others. These conversations can help remind us that we are not alone while we face the uncertainties of death.

Many of us have fears related to death and dying. It can be difficult and even painful, but talking about our fears and concerns is an important part of dealing with death. When we fear what is out of our control, we may cause ourselves and those around us unnecessary heartache. Simply talking about our concerns with our loved ones can comfort us and make us feel less scared.

Important Conversations

The fears we carry from our past and the anticipation of what may be our future can prevent patients and caregivers from experiencing special moments of meaningful interaction. We may hesitate to have important conversations because we fear they may cause our loved ones or ourselves pain. In my experience, the pain of regret is far worse. Once death has come, there are no second chances. When death is imminent, we must do our best to summon our courage before it's too late.

Getting Current

There is no better time to get current with someone than today, but the problem is that we have the illusion of tomorrow. We know tomorrow is not guaranteed, but that doesn't necessarily stop us from depending on its existence. Death has a way of shaking us out of this illusion; it forces us to accept that we can no longer put off the things that we would rather say and do tomorrow. If we are granted the providential moment to refresh and restore before a death, we would be wise to take it.

This might seem like an overwhelming call to action, but when we get to the heart of what is really important, it's not nearly as complicated as our worried minds would have us believe.

The most personal experience I've had with Hospice was in 1998 when my father was dying from heart problems and a series of strokes which left him completely paralyzed. We cared for dad in the living room of my home, for one week, before his death. The whole family was there and involved in his care. Up until the day of his death, dad was fully aware of his condition, and of all those around him. The last week of his life, he was unable to move any part of his body, and was unable to speak. He was only able to see, hear, blink, and shed tears.

About two months prior, before his health rapidly declined, I had gone to visit my dad. We talked for at least forty-five minutes about work, his grandkids, and some of his regrets in life. I don't remember how our goodbyes went that day, if we hugged or said I love you.

To this day, eighteen years after his death, my memories from the last week of his life are good ones. We were lucky to share that special and sacred time together. I was able to express to him the things that mattered most, and I was able to do so more than once. I asked him to forgive me for any pain I had caused him and I let him know that I forgave him for the pain he had caused me. I thanked him for the manifold acts of love he had given me in my lifetime. I told him, "I love you," and I assured him that I would always remember him. Dad was able to respond not with words or a strong hug, but with blinks and tears that communicated his love and acceptance. Those last moments with dad were both precious and painful. I am grateful to have had that experience for many reasons.

During the months and years that followed, there were moments when my thoughts would get the best of me and I found myself agonizing over the things I wished I had said, questions I should have asked while I had the chance, gestures of affection I could have given while he was still alive—sometimes the list seemed endless. Many people I've talked with have gone through this disheartening ordeal themselves; it seems to be a natural part of the bereavement process. I know how fortunate I was to be able to express my feelings to my father, and though there are things I wish I had said, it brings me great comfort to know that I did the best I could in the moment to share my true feelings with him before he passed.

It is so important to make the effort to get current in our relationships while we have the chance. Death may come for anyone at any time and though it might be painful or make us feel vulnerable, it is worth it to let our loved ones know what is in our hearts before it's too late.

Please forgive me

I forgive you

Thank you

I love you

~ Dr. Ira Byock
The Four Things That Matter Most

Needs of the Dying Person

This chapter is meant to be a resource for family members and caregivers as they navigate the many challenges and responsibilities of caring for a dying person.

No two lives are identical and therefore no two deaths are the same. We experience life as unique individuals and yet, we are so very similar: we share the same creator, the same fundamental anatomy, and we all need the same life sustaining elements such as food, water, air, and shelter. How we prioritize and interpret those needs may vary widely from person to person, but when facing end-of-life situations certain needs must be addressed.

A question I will often ask family and other caregivers is "what concerns you most during this difficult time?" The most common answers center around the comfort and care of the person dying, often followed by a sense of urgency to "get it right," say goodbye, and ensure the dying person is content throughout the process as much as possible.

Physical Needs: Providing Care and Managing Pain

At the end of life many people want to be cared for by the people who know them best and love them the most. Often, family are the first choice for this responsibility, however, for various reasons this is not always the case.

This was the situation with one hospice patient I helped care for. The patient's primary caregiver was a friend who lived in the same building. Their close proximity and bond of friendship made this person the ideal caregiver in the dying man's eyes, even though he had living family members. Above all, the patient wanted to maintain his privacy and his friend took this responsibility very seriously. Thanks to his friend, he was able to die on his terms; he received care specific to his needs and wishes, and he died privately in his bed, in the comfort of his own home.

Physical pain is something many dread as death approaches. Whether the pain is foreboding or present, physical or emotional, all efforts to bring relief should be acted upon as soon as possible. When pain has control of the situation all other means of support will be eminently hindered.

Medications of today are numerous and can help minimize physical pain, breathing difficulties, and anxiety. When a patient's pain is not being managed effectively, it can overwhelm the patient's other senses and put additional strain on caregivers. Often times it is difficult to focus on other pressing matters when pain is in the spotlight. It is important to determine how big of a role physical pain is playing and how much it is effecting the patient's quality of life. It is also important to keep in mind that individuals handle physical pain differently, so there is no one medicine or treatment plan that will work for everyone.

A woman who was acting as caregiver for her dying brother explained to me the struggle she felt during her brother's final days. Her brother was in pain the last three days of his life. He would only take small amounts of medication. He wanted to be fully aware of everyone around him. If anyone tried to give him more medicine to help manage his pain, he would turn his head in refusal. Several weeks before his death, during one of their first conversations as caregiver and recipient, the patient had explained to his younger sister that he didn't want to die in pain, like their father did twenty years ago. The sister then asked her brother to tell her what he needed from her. He expressed how grateful he was for her presence; her simply being there was a great comfort to him. With the help of the hospice staff, she did her very best to balance his determination to be fully present and his desire for a pain free death.

Fortunately, this brother and sister were able to talk about formidable but important needs and concerns during this difficult time. The lessons they learned while caring for their father at the end of his life had given them valuable insight into what would be a significantly effectual journey for both of them—twenty years later.

When discussing medications and treatment plans, remember that part of a doctor's job is to help patients and their caregivers make the best decisions for their care. It's okay to ask questions and express concerns, especially if a treatment isn't clear or a medication carries potential worrisome side-effects. If a patient is uncertain or uncomfortable with a specific medication or treatment, help them express their concerns to their doctor and the supporting medical staff as soon as possible.

SEVERE PAIN MANAGEMENT

In certain situations, terminal sedation may be considered as a last resort. This treatment is administered when other palliative treatments are not sufficiently effective, which aims to keep a severely suffering patient unconscious while in the proximity of death. When the concerns of those involved at bedside are for comfort and relief of unendurable pain, (without causing death) this is a solemn decision that must be weighed carefully with the help of the medical professionals involved in the patient's care.

EMOTIONAL AND SPIRITUAL NEEDS

As unique individuals, we all hold different values and beliefs. We cannot assume to know what is in another person's heart any more than we would want someone to assume what is in our own heart. When hoping to fulfil the emotional and spiritual needs of someone who is dying, it is important to try to find out their hopes, desires, and spiritual needs sooner rather than later.

As a chaplain, part of my responsibility is to find out what things are most important to each individual as they face their own mortality. I will often ask them questions to help them get clear on what they want their experience to be. How do they want their last moments to be? Do they want their hand held? Who do they want at their bedside? After asking one woman these questions, she shared a very specific and personal vision for how she wanted to die. She wanted to be surrounded by her family, and when the time came she wanted them to wheel her out to the front porch so she could look out on the ocean one last time. After she shared her ideal scenario with me, I asked her if it would be okay to have her family ask her the same question. She agreed. After I left, they had the conversation and a few days later the family gathered around their beloved mother and grandmother as she took her last breath of the ocean breeze and her last gaze of the ocean she loved so dearly.

Her family clearly loved her very much, and that special conversation allowed them to understand her true wishes and the comfort of knowing that they were able to fulfill them.

Maintaining Autonomy

With each new day, we hope to make our own choices to do what we feel is important. We learn early in life how rewarding and satisfying the experience of doing something for ourselves can be. I often see the process played out with my grandkids. By the age of three, they are persistently determined to do certain things for themselves, or at least make the attempt to do them. This is no different during the period at the end of our lives. We often associate our ability to do things for ourselves as directly connected to our self-worth and sense of control.

Control is our common need for everyday survival. We trust more and risk less with a sense of control. Some find comfort and less of a need for control with faith and knowledge in a sovereign God. With the approach of end-of-life we face our deepest tension, suffering, and feelings of powerlessness.

> *But as for me, I trust in you, O Lord; I say, "You are my God."*
>
> PSALM 31:14

When a person's existence and future is threatened, and death may be imminent, they begin to experience a process of unavoidable losses. During this process, people most often see their abilities and needs transition from self-reliance to dependency. For most, this is a difficult transition and journey. During this end-of-life journey there is a transcendent need for family, friends, neighbors, and community.

We can help our loved ones maintain a sense of control while facing their impending death by asking them a few simple questions. What do you want to accomplish today? What new goals do you have today? Do you feel like doing _____ today?

As disease -or simply the natural aging process- takes control of the human body, mind, and soul, the losses a person experiences will vary. No matter the sum, every loss should be attended to with honesty, love, and compassion. We must not withhold the fact that they are dying, or consider them damaged and diminished as human beings.

I will always remember (as long as I have my memory) a patient I visited with weekly as a chaplain. I learned much from this man. He allowed me to visit with him on a weekly basis for eight months. When I first met this patient, he was able to ambulate from bed to his favorite chair for our visits. The patient's illness slowly but aggressively attacked his physical ability to walk, and eventually he lost the ability to move his legs and arms altogether. During our earlier visits, we mainly talked about God. He expressed his understanding of, and beliefs regarding God. In the eight months when I visited the patient he was alert, ready and able to converse with full cognitive ability; though physically his body was in decline. As we got to know each other better, he shared many meaningful stories from his life with me.

On my last visit with him, he was unable to open his eyes or speak. During that visit, I thanked him for our time together and expressed my gratitude for every conversation we shared and all of the things he taught me. He wasn't able to respond in a way I could see. I hope he knew I was there, and was able to hear me. Two days later he passed away. I was told he enjoyed our time together not so much for spiritual reasons, but because he was able to talk about things that were important to him. He was able to have control over the sharing of his life experiences that were meaningful to him and gave him a sense of accomplishment. I'll be forever grateful for the insights he shared with me.

> *There is a pattern of behavior well-known to those who work with the dying and their families: people die as they live-intensified. Nice people get nicer, busy people get busier, even if only in their dreams. Quiet people get quieter, demanding people demand more. Manipulators will surpass their past controlling behavior.*
>
> ~ MAGGIE CALLAHAN, *Final Gifts*

WHAT TO EXPECT

People tend to die as they live. This is critically important for caregivers, family, and friends to understand, because to expect the behavior of a dying person to be significantly different from what it was earlier in the person's life is unrealistic and can cause undue frustration.

PATIENT NEEDS—A QUICK REFERENCE

A quick reference to help as a guide when dying gets complicated.

- Affirm personal relationships—get them current whenever possible.

- Live as fully as possibly, each day—continue making cherished memories for all to hold onto.

- Start, and continue, the difficult but needed conversations regarding the dying process.

- Allow caregivers to accept and process at their own pace.

- Allow denial to play its role as a coping tool.

- Keep the hard work of loving, and conversation, open.

- Ask and answer questions honestly and respectfully.

- Allow your caregivers to share with you the precious experience of giving and receiving love.

- The dying process starts with the diagnosis. What follows may vary with each person. Each person's unique journey of acceptance is special and completely normal.

- The desire to forgive and forget is good practice, especially at end-of-life. All differences are better off resolved, when possible.

- Assuming the needs of family and caregivers can lead to confusion, mistakes, grief, blame, regret, and anxiety. Be specific.

- Be open and brave with asking and sharing how the bedside scene should be.

- Share your concerns for your family and friends. Tell them anything that you want to tell them while you are still able.

- Remember: I love you, forgive me, I forgive you, and thank you.

These are just a few important things to say—you may have some of your own to say.

Needs of the Caregivers

This chapter focuses on the needs of caregivers. Though the primary focus will always be on the person who is dying, it is also important to understand and acknowledge the needs of the various family and friends who may be responsible for providing end of life care.

CAREGIVING TOGETHER

When multiple people are involved in providing supportive care for someone they love who is dying, it is not likely that everyone involved will always be on the same page. Maybe they can agree on pain management, but can't agree on who is best suited to fulfill certain supportive rolls. Some people may shut down completely, consumed by feelings of helplessness and sorrow while others have a seemingly endless well of optimism. To help facilitate open and honest dialogue, here are a few things to keep in mind.

1. Everyone deals with death differently both inwardly and outwardly. Do not expect everyone to express their emotions in the same manner.

2. If someone is struggling, they may lash out at others, especially those they feel most comfortable around. When emotions run high, it can be helpful to call a time-out and let everyone involved gather their thoughts.

3. Do not take it personally when there is a disagreement. Avoid placing blame on others and try to find common ground.

4. Remember that the most important thing is ensuring the care and comfort of the person who is preparing to transition from life to death.

All any of us can do is our best, be ourselves, and allow others to come alongside us. Everyone needs help when walking others through the valley of the shadow of death and when it's time for each of us to take our walk, we will indeed need others to help us on our way.

Telling Your Story

When talking with the bereaved as they struggle with regrets and sorrow, I will often ask them if they are beating themselves up over something that can't be changed. If they tried in earnest to understand and honor the needs, emotions, and desires of their loved one, then they can take comfort in the fact that they did the best they could at the time, with the tools and information available to them.

Sometimes, anticipatory grief can get in the way of our ability to act as caregivers. Perhaps important things were left unsaid, or words were spoken in anger. We may look back on how we handled a difficult situation and recognize that we fell short of our own expectations. Self-reflections such as these can cause incredible pain. This is especially true after a death, because the finality of death leaves no room for second chances. Feelings of regret and shame can stay with us for months, years, even our whole lives. However, though our loved ones may no longer be physically with us, it is never too late to forgive ourselves for our own shortcomings. People make mistakes, it's part of being human. We can't change the past, but we can carry the lessons we learn from our mistakes into the future; allowing the light of our experiences to shine on ourselves and others through life's many challenges.

We do the best we can at the end of ones' life, with the tools and understanding we have at the time. Rarely, if ever, does dying seem to end perfectly for those left with grief. Contentment may be elusive and difficult to find. Continue searching; keep sharing your experience with those willing to listen. By talking and telling your story you will increase your opportunity to find peace, resolve, meaning, and contentment. By telling your story you will impart knowledge to others; lessons learned that will help them to uncomplicate the challenges faced during the dying process. Your story is a meaningful and significant connection that bonds all humans as we seek to mollify death.

CAREGIVER NEEDS—A QUICK REFERENCE

A quick reference to help as a guide when dying gets complicated.

- Affirm personal relationships—get them current whenever possible.

- Live as fully as possibly, each day—continue making cherished memories for all to hold onto.

- Enable the dying person to be themselves until the end. They are still a human being as they are dying.

- Help to maintain a sense of optimism by offering support and comfort.

- Start, and continue, the difficult but needed conversations regarding the dying process.

- Allow the patient to accept and process at their own pace.

- Allow denial to play its role as a coping tool.

- Keep the hard work of loving, and conversation, open.

- Ask and answer questions honestly and respectfully.

- Talk openly *with* the dying person, not *about* them, or without them.

- Allow the patient the opportunity to complete their life; be mindful of over protecting them and do not avoid the fact that they are dying.

- The dying process starts with the diagnosis. What follows may vary with each person. Be supportive through the dying person's unique journey of acceptance.

- The dying person's long-term goals and outlook will shift to moment by moment relevance. Be aware as you look to meet their needs as they live in this new state of being. Plan with them, keeping in mind their time table.

- Be flexible, as needs may change throughout the process.

- The desire to forgive and forget is good practice, especially at end-of-life. All differences are better off resolved, when possible.

- Assuming the needs of the dying person can lead to confusion, mistakes, grief, blame, regret, and anxiety. Be specific.

- Give permission to die, they may be ready but they may need to know for sure that you're ready.

- Assure the dying that you will be fine—as a family, relationally, emotionally, physically, financially, and spiritually.

- Ask the dying to share their concerns for you and others. They need to know that you will continue in life well.
- I love you, forgive me, I forgive you, thank you, and I will always remember you.

These are just a few important things to say—you may have some of your own to say.

Lessons from a Hospice Chaplain

A hospice chaplain provides emotional and spiritual support to terminally ill patients and their families. They are trained to help comfort and guide people through grief, illness, and death.

In my many years as a chaplain, I have had the honor and privilege of helping numerous people navigate the murky waters that we must all sail through when experiencing death, whether it is our own or someone we love. My hope is to make the dying process less complicated, with some simple lessons and ideas learned from others as they endured this unavoidable journey to death.

Comfort

One patient I will never forget was facing a difficult illness and a difficult dying process. Before I met this patient, her nurse explained to me the patient's prognosis and the symptoms of her disease, as well as the patient's spiritual, mental, and emotional state-of-being. The nurse also advised me to wear protective gloves, a medical gown, and mask.

The patient had requested a chaplain visit. As we exchanged greetings there was an obvious expression of uneasiness which she wanted to put to rest right away. She wanted to apologize for the symptoms of her illness. One of the symptoms was a very strong odor. The door to her private room was kept closed and a special ventilation system had been installed to extract the odor as much as possible. The patient was suffering from multiple symptoms that made each day almost intolerable for her. During each visit, she wanted to talk about her faith in God and her love for her family. She talked about dying, and how she knew that it would be soon. She liked having scriptures read to her, and was comforted with prayer.

Every time I visited her, there was an obvious look of malicious harshness imprinted on her face due to the aggressive progression of her disease. The morning she died, I saw her only minutes after she passed away. The nurse had called the Chaplains office for a chaplain visit because the patient's death appeared imminent. As I entered her room and looked to greet her, she was still, breathless, and lifeless. It was clear she was no longer here; no longer in pain, no longer in discomfort, and no longer in need. An unusual thing happened after she died, and I asked the nurse to confirm the change I observed in the patient's facial expression. To this day, I have never seen such an expression of peace and relief, as was in her smile, after a death. The nurse, smiling, agreed. The patient's eyes were closed and her smile stayed in place for hours; it was still there when her family came to say their goodbyes.

> *She didn't die at home,*
>
> *With family to attend and carefully comb,*
>
> *She died with gleaming hope and peace;*
>
> *She has now life that will never cease.*
>
> *She will forever, now, be at peace.*
>
> ~ Chaplain Garry Hodges

I am always grateful when I can provide comfort to someone facing an imminent death. Though I had no power to ease this woman's physical discomfort, or treat the symptoms of her illness, I was able to comfort her through conversation, prayer, and companionship.

FINDING PEACE

A peaceful death can take place under the best and the worst circumstances. Each one of us is imputed with the privileged affirmation to travel our road of choice, as we journey towards that imposing day.

I've often shared the story of a friend's last wishes given to her paid caregiver just hours before death separated her from her body. This caregiver shared with me the details of one of their last conversations. The caregiver noticed that she was having some difficulty breathing, so she asked my friend if she needed any medication to make her more comfortable. My friend's response; "No honey I'm fine, I know it won't be long now, I want to be fully aware when that time comes. I want to see Jesus and all the Angels that are with Him as He takes me home."

My friend was able to make her wishes known, with support from family and staff. She was fortunate to have control and to feel a sense of purpose in the final act of her life. Each of our final moments will be different in many ways. We must face the complex and difficult circumstances before us with resolve, courage, compassion, and hard work. The final moments of a person's life will leave us with memories of sadness and joy for the rest of our lives.

"Passed away peacefully, at home, with family present"—a phrase commonly stated by loved ones, as they eulogize the deceased in the obituary section of the newspaper. The three components: peacefully, at home, and with family, are desirable qualities for most of us as we face death, and its finality. Maybe, these statements help us make sense of, add value to, and bring meaning to our own lives, as we search for the strength to continue living after a loved one leaves this world.

When you read someone's obituary that doesn't include *peacefully, at home, with family,* does this mean the deceased is unable to be at peace? I certainly hope not! These three qualities do not apply in every circumstance, but that does not mean a person cannot find peace at the end of their life. As we saw with the terribly sick patient mentioned earlier, her illness did not allow her to be at peace in the time leading up to her death. However, once she died, the terrible symptoms of her disease no longer plagued her, and she was able to be at peace. Sometimes "home" is not the ideal location for someone to be cared for at the end of their life. When a hospice environment is available at end-of-life, we may feel supported and empowered to spend more time sharing stories, resolving unfinished business, and expressing precious emotions as we walk our loved ones to the gate on their journey to the other side.

TIMELINES

We are given clues, signs, and symptoms to help determine when a life may end. These precursors can be helpful for loved ones and caregivers, but other times they can be misleading. The prognosis that estimates an imminent end may prompt loved ones to preemptively seek closure. The prognosis that estimates a longer timeline before death may cause patients and families to put off important matters for another day, only to have the patient die sooner than expected. Whenever possible, begin planning and having significant conversations sooner rather than later.

As Bereavement Coordinator for hospice I've had many follow up conversations with loved ones over days, weeks, months, and sometimes years after a death. All too often people tell me that the time went by too quickly, leaving many unanswered questions and unresolved issues.

A daughter once tearfully shared that she took off from work for a week to be with her dying father, but he died before she arrived. When I asked if her family had expected him to die so soon, she confided that she was the only one who wasn't ready, and she didn't realize it until it was too late.

A woman told me about the day she and her husband met with his doctor and were told that he had days, weeks, maybe two months to live, but that it was more likely a matter of weeks. She said her husband didn't cry at the news, but she did. The prognosis was given August 10th, he died September 7th, just four weeks later.

Four weeks sounds like plenty of time while on vacation, and for many other situations in life. How much time will you need to prepare yourself, and the people you care about for your final moments of life? When I was younger and healthier, the thought of preparing myself and others for death was inconceivable, unlikely to happen anytime soon. Such thinking could only be awakened by the death of someone else, and then it would be put back in its place—not me not now. Sadly, and unexpectedly, people die; sometimes after we say goodbye, and sometimes before. We don't know how life is going to end for any of us. Inevitably our last day will leave an impression on countless other people for years, and perhaps for eternity.

A man shared how important hospice care had been for his wife. They had been together forty-five years. Hospice care had helped extend his wife's life, allowing him eleven more months with her, eleven more months to make arrangements, eleven more months for her to prepare him for her death. Those extra months were precious and life changing for this man and he was incredibly grateful.

Seeing as Believing

Because we live by sight, we have the miraculous ability to always hope for the best regarding life's many ordeals. The everyday reassurance of what has been seen and experienced allows us to hope for those same things to continue unhindered by life's obstacles. Our reliance upon sight is both natural and normal.

> *This I recall to my mind, therefore I have hope.*
>
> Lamentations 3:21

When a human being begins the transition from this life, there begins something beyond the norm. There can be moments that seem to make little or no sense to those watching and listening. This transitional experience may be brief, or it may take a lingering course. When a person is on what seems to be a lingering trajectory, without any purpose or understanding, I will encourage those around them to see this time as the most important final event in the dying person's life.

For the dying, this is not an irrelevant byway, but a passage of great importance on their journey. What is taking place during this time may have been repressed, forgotten, or postponed throughout their lifetime. I believe this is an important part of the dying process. Mistakenly, we may refer to them during this time in their life as confused, non-responsive, comatose, disoriented, or hallucinating. However we see it, wouldn't it be wonderful to know their experience and be able to respond? More importantly, this is their time to complete their life journey with uninterrupted contemplation, reconciliation, awareness, and celestial sightings.

During the writing of this booklet, a friend shared a story with me about one of the last conversations she had with her grandmother before she passed. Her grandmother was suffering from Alzheimer's and the disease had advanced to the point where she could barely speak, and she no longer recognized even her closest family members. The family was mourning the loss of their beloved matriarch. Even though her physical death was not immediately imminent, the woman they knew and loved seemed all but gone. The granddaughter explained that after spending just a few minutes in her grandma's room, she looked at her with crystal clear recognition and called her closer to her bedside. No one could have anticipated what would happen next.

The grandmother addressed her granddaughter not by her name, but by the name of her childhood playmate, Ellie. She excitedly began to ask "Ellie" all sorts of questions about experiences they had when they were small children. The granddaughter had never heard of Ellie, and was initially confused, but she had a feeling her grandmother was not simply rambling incoherently, but rather she was sharing precious details of her life, details no one in the room had ever heard before. She encouraged her grandmother to continue with her stories and she spent the next twenty minutes speaking clearly and vibrantly to her family, regaling them all with memories, funny stories, and happy moments from her youth. For a brief time, the woman was not consumed by her disease, and the family had their grandma back.

We take the entire course of our lives with us into the final months and weeks.

~ ROBERT J. KASTENBAUM
Death, Society, and Human Experience

WHAT MAKES END-OF-LIFE DIFFICULT?

Though being a commonplace and familiar part of life, death is often ignored, evaded, and kept at a distance with hopes that it will occur later, at a more acceptable time. The difficulties we experience during the process of death and dying are common and shared by every person, family, community, nation, and culture.

The difficulties and complications of death are among life's most wearisome challenges. Everything that was once normal seems demolished; life, with great abruptness, is now anything but ordinary. It may sound strange, but these feelings of upheaval are completely normal.

Our emotions, needs, actions, and reactions are common to our nature as human beings. You are not alone, you are normal! Our reaction to death is very much normal, because death is not the normal part of life. Death, in essence, is the separation of body and soul of the human being. The tearing apart of body and soul is what makes death so difficult, complicated, and in many ways troubling. Fear of the unknown, loss of control, suffering, finality, the separation of loved ones, and the enigma of what comes next can all leave a person feeling overwhelmed and hopeless.

Uncomplicating Death

Death may separate my soul, my anatomy;

From this world and my family,

With faith, it's only temporary.

My hope in Christ, now binary.

Death may seem now, as, my leaving;

Let it be seen as my arriving.

In life and now in death;

Where there, ends my breath;

I have much depth and breadth.

No longer is life, without;

Nor will I be, left out.

No longer without meaning;

Now, there is much gleaning.

No longer a need to pre-purpose;

My destination is now my purpose.

No longer need hope, for my future;

Let this not be just a rumor;

Your future, may come sooner.

~ CHAPLAIN GARRY HODGES

Life, Love, and Tomorrow

Life has many rewards and difficulties. It is a continuous series of lessons and tests. The last and greatest test we will face during our lifetime is physical death. There are many reasons that make death so difficult. It separates us, it appears to be final, it allows for only one chance to do it well, it may be painful, it may take too long; the list of reasons could be its own book.

Love may be the thing that makes death most difficult to deal with for both the surviving family and the dying person. Love is our greatest reward in life. When death is imminent, a source of giving and receiving love seems to be at risk. There is no substitute for having our loved ones with us, but death does not have to be the end of a relationship. The love we have for people who leave this world before us does not die with them. We can carry them with us by remembering them, sharing their stories, even speaking to them or thinking to ourselves "what would they advise me to do in this situation?" when we wish they were there to ask for advice.

> *Who they were, is who they will always be.*
>
> ~ CHAPLAIN GARRY HODGES

For those of you who have lost a loved one and have been struggling with doubts and regrets, beating yourself up over something that you've done, or wish that you had done. If each new day your list of regrets continues to grow regarding these things, my hope for you is to stop! Stop tearing yourself up over these feelings. More importantly learn from your experiences; you may have the sacred opportunity someday to comfort and support another soul during their time of adversity. Continue to live your life and never stop growing. You have much to give, don't stop now.

Grief, Pain and Sorrow Is There No Tomorrow?

Don't live this day grieving in pain and sorrow,

As if, there is no tomorrow.

Let not your loss be only seen in Sorrow;

Let others see and know the love

Which gave you hope for Tomorrow.

Live not as if there is no tomorrow,

Today be my hope for tomorrow.

Do not lose this day in sorrow,

Many need your love, they also have

Much pain and sorrow.

Let grief, pain, and sorrow no longer

Rob you this day or tomorrow,

Let others see and know there is

Much love and hope,

Today and Tomorrow.

~ Chaplain Garry Hodges

> *We cannot make sure that the Lord will instantly remove all disease from those we love, but we can know that believing prayer for the sick is far more likely to be followed by restoration than anything else in the world; and where this does not avail, we must meekly bow to His will by who life and death are determined. The tender heart of Jesus waits to hear our griefs. Let's pour them into His patient ear.*
>
> ~ Charles H. Spurgeon

A Note From the Author

When I was eight I had my first memorable experience while visiting my grandmother. My family and I flew from California to Raleigh, North Carolina, to see her for what would be the last time. She was dying from cancer and my memories of visiting her while on her death bed are still with me to this day. Though she was bedbound, weak, and in need of twenty-four-hour care, she was alert and grateful for our visit. In the precious few days we were with her, Grandma shared her love with us as we gathered around her bed in her small, dark, one room apartment. She died a few days after we returned home to California. She was the only grandma I had known and that visit was only the third time I had been in her presence.

That final experience with her may well have planted the seed deep within me and continues to drive me as a chaplain to offer support, comfort, hope, and peace to those during their end-of-life journey.

Acknowledgements

Twenty-eight years as a hospital chaplain, retirement facility chaplain, hospice chaplain, and bereavement coordinator continue to reaffirm my purpose and reason for my time on this earth. I am so grateful for the training I have received from other healthcare professionals, everyone who has trusted me and allowed me the opportunity to care for others, and all I have learned from the many conversations I've had at the bedside of the dying, and with many family members and caregivers. Each and every day in their presence offers me a new opportunity for a special didactic lesson, and a time for growth and reflection.

Notes

Notes

Notes

www.ingramcontent.com/pod-product-compliance
Lightning Source LLC
Chambersburg PA
CBHW021136300426
44113CB00006B/458